DAMAGED
Goods

DONNA M. BARNES

Donna M. Barnes

Copyright © 2020 by Donna M. Barnes
All rights reserved. This book or any portion thereof
may not be reproduced or used in any manner whatsoever
without the express written permission of the publisher
except for the use of brief quotations in a book review.
Printed in the United States of America
First Printing, 2020
ISBN 978-0-578-74809-2

Table of Contents

Introduction

Chapter 1
The Beginning 3

Chapter 2
The BIG Move 9

Chapter 3
Abort 16

Chapter 4
Masked 22

Chapter 5
How to Love 26

Chapter 6
Damaged Beyond Repair 35

Chapter 7
Total Knock Out (TKO) 40

Chapter 8
Blessing in Disguise 50

Chapter 9
Finding Me 54

Chapter 10
All of Me..*59*

Chapter 11
Until Death Do Us Part.......................................*64*

Conclusion

Damaged *Goods*

Introduction

Life isn't always as it seems.
...sometimes, it's totally different.
As a child, I dreamed, and I dreamed big. I often dreamed of growing up and couldn't wait until I did. Little did I know, being grown wasn't for me.

One of my biggest dreams was to become a successful lawyer, able to afford all of the luxuries my heart desired, including hire a maid and staff to run my mansion, in Washington, D.C. My massive home would come equipped with pristine landscaping and greenery, in spite of the fact that I never developed an appreciation for the great outdoors. I wanted a round driveway with a black limousine parked in it. And since I didn't want to drive it myself, I'd hire someone to do that for me, too.

Basically, if someone else could do what I didn't feel like doing, I believed God wanted me to pay them to do it for me. That's why he created them, right? In addition, I'd have five children and a husband to enjoy my riches. I was only seven-years-old but I knew exactly what I wanted, how I wanted my life to be and I was going to get it. I didn't mind working to get what I desired, and certainly didn't mind dreaming of success.

But what happens when you wake up and the dreams you had as a child still haven't manifested? What happens when life doesn't go as planned or the way you intended? I had no idea life doesn't play out to our wants. At seven, I couldn't recognize God's plan or understand the concept of it. I consumed with my own plan. And as for those big dreams rocking me to sleep at night? Well things were about to be shaken up.

Damaged Goods

The Beginning

"**You weren't planned, you were a mistake.**"

Believe it or not, more children have heard those words than you'd think. Often, parents say things without given thought to the psychological effects it can have on a child. "Sticks and stones may break my bones, but words will never hurt me," is the biggest lie ever told. Words hurt. We must guard our speech, because words can't be taken back. We can apologize and attempt to right our wrongs, but we can't undo the hurt our word cause.

How do I know all of this? Experience. I wasn't part of the life my parents planned for themselves. According to them, I wasn't even supposed to be exist. Do you know what it feels like to lose your identity before you've had the chance to develop one? When I was conceived, I wasn't wanted. I entered this world a rejected child. Before my heart was fully developed, it was preparing to be broken.

Already having three children, my mother considered aborting me. Thinking of me wasn't about what color she'd paint my nursery or who'd throw her a baby shower, things most expectant moms look forward to doing. The joy my mother should have felt about my conception was overruled by despair.

"What am I going to do with a fourth child?"

Obviously, she decided to keep me. Not only did she decide to keep me, but she took care of me. She fed me and made sure all my needs were met. What my mother didn't know all those years ago, was the very child she had considered aborting, would be the child to make the biggest difference.

The unwanted child would grow up to break generational curses.

I wasn't wanted, but I had a purpose. I wish I could say discovering my history was the biggest challenge of my life, but it was just the first of many obstacles I'd face. I was birthed into a dysfunctional family, which only added to the many other challenge's life hurled at me.

I didn't grow up with my father. Unlike my mother, who stuck it out and did the best she could to raise us, he took another path…one that didn't include me or my siblings. His absence felt like another slap in the face. Another rejection and another heartbreak, from the two people who should have loved me the most. How many more heartbreaks could one take?

When will it end?

Even after all these years, I can't hear the song, "Dance With my Father", without tears flooding my eyes, because I've never experienced that bond with my own. It would be a pleasure to dance with him, but an even greater pleasure just to meet him. To talk to him. All the things a daughter shouldn't have to beg for.

Even though my mother birthed four children, I only grew up with one of them, my sister. One of my brothers was kidnapped by his father when he was three years old, devastating my mother. It was years later before I realized my mother was not the only person who had suffered through that loss; it impacted me and my siblings, too. My other brother lived in Louisiana. There were several summers when we'd fly back and forth from Washington D.C to Louisiana; however, those memories are a blur. The mind is an amazing thing. If you try hard enough, it will allow you to block out the bad moments. You try not to remember the pain or the hurt.

You just try to keep going.

I wish I could recall one good memory from my trips to Louisiana, but I can't. When events have traumatized you, the past creeps out of nowhere and reopen the same wounds you felt years ago. Trips to my grandparents' house in Louisiana weren't fun. I don't think anyone's excited to be somewhere they're not wanted.

My grandparents didn't hide the fact they didn't like my sister and me. They talked bad about us, our mother, and treated us differently from everyone else. It was like boot camp; we couldn't even go anywhere. My cousins were able to do the things we couldn't. I don't know if my grandparents' feelings towards us were because of who we were, or how they felt about my mother. I felt like we were paying for her wrongdoings. It's not good knowing you're unwanted. This wasn't the life I was supposed to be living.

Even though my life was filled with unhappiness, it wasn't all bad. Mom worked at a hospital; I loved going to her job and chatting with her coworkers. I even had a crush on one of them. There were also times when Mom would go play bingo; or we were out of school, that my sister and I would go stay at our babysitters' house. We loved the babysitters; they were so much fun. They allowed us to be the typical, energetic kids we were. They did our hair and entertained us, too. Now that I'm older, I believe they loved being around us because we kept them young and active.

For years, Mom managed to take care of us on her own. From the outside looking in, single parents make raising their children look easy, but that's far from the truth. There were times my sister and I would come home from school to find our clothes, furniture, and other belongings on the side of the road. Imagine being a child, watching others dig through your things, and taking them. Shame, guilt, and embarrassment washed over me.

Another low blow.

I was ashamed not because our friends and neighbors knew what happened to us, but I was more ashamed knowing that everything we owned amounted to a small space on the sidewalk. We had no choice but to start over. I'd love to say it never happened again, but unfortunately, it was the first of many evictions. As with all habits, the more you do it, the easier it becomes. Eventually, eviction became our norm. In the midst of all the storms and chaos, my sister and I did have one thing…our freedom. We were able to hang out with our friends and invite people over to visit. During that time, even with all the evictions, my sister and I had no major worries, until the night when everything changed.

My mother had a boyfriend I couldn't stand. Every time he came around, I cringed. He acted like he was my father, but didn't know how strong-willed I was. Whenever he said something I didn't like, I turned cold on him. And he surely would've been dead if looks could indeed kill. But I wasn't the David who would slay Goliath.

One night, my sister and I sat in our room coloring, when we heard a loud thump come from the living room. We looked at each other, then ran to investigate. We froze when we saw his body on the floor, Mom's terrified eyes stared our direction.

"Go back to your room," she yelled.

That night, the giant fell.

Suddenly, my sister and I were rushed out of the house and sent across the hall with neighbors. We didn't have family in Washington, D.C., so we were left with complete strangers as Mom was handcuffed and carried away. She

Damaged *Goods*

was only gone for a couple of days, but those were the scariest two days of my life. I didn't know what was going on or how long she'd be away. What would happen to my sister and me?

When she returned, we found out that Mom's boyfriend hit her, and she stabbed him.

Guess he learned she wasn't the woman to mess with.

As if that's not crazy enough, there was the time when I almost lost my life. My sister and I stayed at our friend's house, and we all decided to go for a swim. The only problem was... I couldn't swim. But my not being able to swim didn't stop us. At first, things were going just fine. We were chilling in the water when for some reason, me-the non-swimmer, thought it would be cool to hop on my friend's back and dive into the water.

Time slowed down as we plopped into the pool. Minutes felt like forever as I sank further and further to the bottom of the water. I believed I was coming up and screaming for help, but in reality, I was still sinking.

I don't know how long I was under water, but I knew I was near death. It was almost the end for me. I can't recall who pulled me out or who gave me CPR. All I knew was that was one mistake I'd never make again. Even today, I'll quickly decline any invitation to go swimming.

Once I recovered, I relayed the news I almost drowned to Mom over the phone. I waited for the hysteria. Was prepared to calm her down and reassure her that I was okay, but she didn't respond as I expected at all.

Mom simply said, "That's good for you."

I couldn't believe it. Didn't she just hear me say I almost drowned? Didn't she understand that I could've died? There was no "I'm sorry that happened to you. Are you okay?" Or "I love you; we'll talk more about this once you get home." Nope, there was none of that. Her empty response would have to do.

Yes, I did wrong by sneaking in the pool, but were my actions so bad that my own mother couldn't show sympathy for one minute? For the life of me, I couldn't wrap my head around her response. How could a mother say that to her child who almost died? No matter how much wrong a child does, he or she still needs to know they're loved. Parents must remember that their words can harm their children.

As a child, you look to your parents as providers. They're almost like superheroes, who can make anything happen. Although I didn't understand then what I know now, Mom's still my superhero. See, parents can only do what's within their ability to do, with the resources available to them. Some things are taught, while others are caught. Learned behavior is a more specific term, to explain why some parents only know how to demonstrate what was demonstrated to them (whether good or bad), while others avoid treating their children the way they were as kids.

I realize now, I expected too much. I'd ask myself how a parent could do this, or that, not truly understanding half the things happening in mine or my mother's life. I didn't consider what Mom was going through. I just knew something was going on. Something was happening.

But it wasn't too long before…

Damaged *Goods*

The BIG Move

We were evicted again.
This eviction, unlike the rest, was extremely different. Not only was it the last eviction, but my mother was also fired from her job at the VA hospital after ten years. It was the only job she'd had; our only source of income. That was the only job she had. Her only way to bring in income.

What were we going to do now?

During past evictions, we'd move to another place. Not this time. Moving requires money; since Mom lost her job, we didn't have any. This transition was BIG and detrimental. Not only did this change affect my mother, but it affected my sister and me as well.

I was relieved when Mom mentioned one of her good friends would allow us to live with her in Washington D.C. Once we settled in, things seemed to be going so well. At least we thought they were. At the end of the school year, Mom dropped a major bomb on us.

"I am going to stay in Washington D.C. and you two are moving to Virginia with your brother's father and his wife."

The news hit me like a sucker punch.

I was entering the 6th grade next school year, and didn't want to move to Virginia. Granted, it wasn't as far as Louisiana, but it may as well have been. Not to mention relocating would put too many miles between my mother and me. I didn't want to leave her, she and my sister – were all I knew.

Why were we being ripped apart?

I tried hard to convince myself separating wasn't a big deal. That we'd moved before, and I should stop fussing and just go along with the plan, but no matter how many times I said it, I still didn't believe it. Not only was I being forced to leave my mother, I had to go to another state. Considering Mom worked long hours, played a lot of Bingo and left us with babysitters from time to time, we didn't spend much time with her anyway. Still, all I wanted was her.

All I needed was to be with her.

I begged and pleaded to stay with Mom, but she felt moving was best. I'm fairly sure, Mom felt she was doing what she had to do, but I didn't interpret it that way. To me, *what was best* looked like rejection. Again. Since she didn't abort me, Mom was rejecting me. I couldn't father why she couldn't just get another job so we could all be together. Why didn't she fight to keep us? I wanted to scream, "I'm your daughter, fight for me"!"

Have you ever yearned for someone who was close in proximity but emotionally far away?

As much as I fought it, the BIG day arrived.

In spite of my best efforts, my sister and I were shipped to Virginia. Sometimes, even when you know it's coming, the magnitude of change takes you by surprise. And sometimes it takes a while before reality hits. Life in Virginia was alright for a while. But I yearned to be with Mom. Things were rough for us, but at least we were together.

Damaged *Goods*

September rolled around, and my sister and I enrolled in middle school in Cumberland, Va. I made friends at my new school, but we weren't able to go to any of our friend's homes. In fact, most activities we were allowed to do while living with Mom came to a complete stop.

Adjusting to our new life was overwhelming. We talked to Mom every now and then, but weren't allowed to call her too often. As the days passed, we got more adjusted. At first, my brother's stepmother was nice, but over time she changed. I felt like she had it out for me, but not my sister. What I failed to notice was I was the cause of her attitude towards me.

I'm known for speaking my mind. Well I was the same way as a child. I was actually worse back then, because whatever hit my mind slipped out my mouth. No filter, no sugarcoating. She never disciplined me, however, I overheard our guardians fussing about my smart mouth and behaviors. My brother's father whipped me for acting out, and by all rights I should have been disciplined. The thing is, I felt if I was going to get whipped, it should've been my own father, not my brother's.

The scripture says, "Trouble don't last always". In my case, it seemed like it did. I was constantly in trouble. At first, I only got into trouble at home, but soon I messed up at school, too. No one understood why I behaved the way I did. I wasn't too sure myself. On the outside, people saw a little girl who wouldn't behave, but on the inside was a terrified child holding onto a shocking secret.

A secret she trusted herself to keep.

Trust is everything. But what happens when your trust is tampered with? When it's broken? What happens when the person who's supposed to be your protector becomes your predator?

One night, after everyone went to bed, my brother's father entered the room my sister and I shared. Thinking I was getting in trouble for something I'd done again, I played sleep. He walked quietly to my bed and stood over me. I thought the BIG move was us moving and uprooting our lives; it was nothing compared to the real BIG move.

The move of my guardian's hands on my thighs.

That night was the first time he touched me inappropriately.

My brother's father molested me.

I glared at him in silence. Wanted so bad to say something, to cry out for help to defend myself. But the words stuck in the back of my throat. He held his finger over his mouth, warning me to not say a word. Silent screams raced through my mind. The irony of everything was that Mom never taught me I wasn't supposed to be touched in the places he touched. I knew it was wrong, though.

And helpless to stop it.

I didn't wake my sister after he left. Didn't even tell her the next day. He acted as if nothing happened, so I did the same. Why worry about it if he wasn't. We continued on, business as usual. I went to school, came home and we interacted the way we normally did. A part of me was in shock. It was easier to pretend everything was fine during the day, but nighttime was the night told a different story. I wasn't sleeping, and made sure I wore long pajama pants and shirts to bed. I tried sleeping closer to my sister, and did whatever it took to keep him from violating me again.

All of my efforts were in vain.

He was a manipulator who conjured other ways to get me. Several nights passed before he entered our room again. This time, he woke me and beckoned for me to exit the room quietly. I didn't want to go with him, but I did. I felt like I didn't have a choice. I was living under his roof, wasn't I? He was providing for me, wasn't he? Heck mom trusted him, so I should trust him too, right?

I was trapped. An 11-year-old child, lost and lonely. My adolescence was stripped from me. My innocence was stolen. Freedom taken away. I was depleted, empty, and numb. I wanted him to stop but I was too scared to do anything about it.

I questioned my silence. Did being quiet mean I wanted it? I could've said no, but then what? I was confused, damaged and depressed- none of which I felt mattered to anyone besides me. It sure did not matter to him. His only concern was finding more hiding places to have his way with me.

Some nights, we'd go to the shed outside the house. Other nights, he'd lay me down in his truck. It was horrible. I can still smell the awful stench of his garlic breath. Those were the nights I barely slept. The abuse wasn't every day, but it happened often enough. Some days when my sister and I got in trouble, she'd get a whipping, but he'd tell me I'd get punished later.

I knew what that meant.

Sometimes I wondered how my sister didn't pick up on what was happening. And how his wife didn't either. Was everybody blind except me? How couldn't they tell? Who could possibly miss how he'd go ballistic whenever I mentioned a boy? Not like an overprotective father, but like a man being cheated on by his woman. I wanted to scream at the top of my lungs, "You're supposed to be my caregiver! You're not supposed to hurt me!" But as usual, I kept quiet. When he and his wife began arguing more, I thought things with me would stop. There was so much confusion in the house, I hoped their fussing was because she discovered the truth about us.

Silly me, I thought I was getting rescued.

It never happened.

I didn't have a superhero.

Why didn't I tell Mom?

Once I mapped everything in my mind, I came to the only conclusion I could: Mom couldn't find out. I didn't have a father, and refused to risk losing the piece of my mother I did have. If I would've confessed to Mom, I knew what the outcome would be. My brother's father would be dead; Mom would be locked up. So, I let things continue even though I knew it was wrong. I didn't even want it to happen; and didn't want him. I was a child, for Pete's sake! I just laid there and let him do what he'd do until he finished and we returned to "normal" life.

I hated asking that man for anything, but sometimes we needed clothes and other necessities and I knew once he bought what I needed, I'd have to give him what he wanted.

Why me?

Why touch me? Why molest me?

He had a wife to share a bed with every night, yet he chose me. I was grateful he didn't mess with my sister, but wondered why he chosen me over her, too.

He kept it up the entire time we lived with him. Our room was right next to him and his wife, so it made it easier for us to overhear them arguing. One night, they had a pretty severe fight about something I'd say. No surprise, since she was always upset about something I said.

"What's wrong?" he asked her.

"She said I need some dick!" his wife hollered.

I burst out laughing, because it was true. I didn't know she overheard me saying that to my sister. They lowered their voices so I couldn't hear what else was said, but I braced for the worst. I knew for sure he was coming to punish me, but thankfully never showed up in our room. The next morning, I heard him talking on the phone, but couldn't make out who he was speaking to or what they were saying. I didn't care, but that phone call was about to alter my life.

Again.

The school year was coming to an end, and so was the molestation. He informed my sister and I, that he was getting divorced, and was taking us to Louisiana to stay with our relatives. He'd already spoken to Mom about it and everything was set. As much as I hated the thought of

Damaged Goods

moving to Louisiana, the thought of spending another day in his house was much worse.

Louisiana was bad, but it couldn't be any worse than anything I'd experienced with him.

Abort

When I die, I know I'm going to heaven because I've already been to hell.

That's what I used to tell myself whenever I reflected on my life. I thought moving would make things better. Proverbs 18:21 states, "Death and life are in the power of the tongue." It's important to be mindful of the words we speak. I wish I would've learned that lesson before I kept complaining about how bad I wanted to move. Out of nowhere came another transition. One I wasn't prepared for. But at least it was a fresh start.

Things couldn't possibly get any worse, right?

Even though life with Mom wasn't the best, I wanted to be with her. At least we'd be together. After finding out I was moving, I knew things wouldn't get better. Call it a gut feeling or maybe it was based on my past experiences. Somehow, I just knew. Even though I didn't expect better, I was blindsided by the worst to come.

I left one form of abuse, just to be subjected to another one. Even though it wasn't the same kind of abuse, abuse is

Damaged *Goods*

abuse. No matter if it's sexual, verbal, emotional, or physical abuse. I had already experienced sexual abuse by my brother's father, someone my mother and I trusted.

After we moved, though I prayed to leave the abuse behind, too… but it followed me. It turned out I did not. The only thing that changed when I moved was the type of abuse and how it occurred.

My personal hell grew deeper and hotter. How could I live through another hell experience, when I was still reeling from the first one?

My days in Louisiana were dark. I'm sure my relatives loved me, but they didn't like me. They weren't strangers, but I hadn't spent enough time with my family to form a true bond. That was fine with me. I didn't know them, and I didn't care to. Louisiana wasn't where I wanted to be, anyway. My daily frown said exactly how I felt. I didn't smile because there was nothing to smile about. Besides, I didn't want anyone thinking I was friendly when I didn't want to be bothered.

All I wanted was to understand WHY.

Why must I endure torture? What could I have possibly done wrong to go through all this? Why couldn't I stay with people I knew, people who were like family, in Washington? Why couldn't I go to my old school and talk or hang with my old friends? Life wasn't fair at all.

I didn't have the strength to dream.

Summer came to an end and I started school at Livonia High. I didn't have many friends, but I did remember some students from elementary school, during temporary stays in Louisiana. I didn't remember their names, just their faces.

My life sucked.

Have you ever felt that way before? Like your life sucks so bad, you're not sure if it will get any better? I didn't want to deal with or live with our family- I just wanted Mom. I would call and beg her to come to Louisiana to get my sister and me, but she hated Louisiana even more than I did. I understood why she didn't want to come, but couldn't believe she'd leave me to live in a place she couldn't even stand to visit.

Unlike some families, my family drama didn't just stay behind closed doors of our house. It seemed that everyone knew our business; my dirty laundry caused the few neighborhood friends I did have to practically shun us. They barely wanted to come to the house. My life wasn't improving at all. Darkness engulfed me, and I desperately needed light. I prayed Mom would be that light for me.

A better life wasn't going to magically appear living in a place where I didn't want to be. At that point I gave up. Success didn't seem attainable, so I didn't apply myself in school. My grades were horrific. Sometimes I'd act out so someone, anyone, would notice me. I needed someone to recognize my pain and acknowledge my hurt, that I was misunderstood. My teachers didn't notice, and neither did my guidance counselor. The adults in my life were failing me. When they did pay attention, they thought I was just "being bad." And my family? Well they were too wrapped up in themselves to notice me. Instead of seeing how much I hated my life, that I was slowly dying, I would get put out of class, sent to the office, and reprimanded for my behavior.

There was no one to help me.

I was drowning in misery and verbal abuse pushed me deeper in despair. I hoped to find refuge in my grandmother, but she was my new abuser. I imagined grandmothers were sweet ladies who baked cookies, gave the best hugs, and served as comforters with words of wisdom that prepped their grandchildren for a fantastic life. At least those were the grandmothers I saw on television.

My grandmother was nothing like them at all. Instead of affirming how beautiful and smart I was, my grandmother would growl, "You ain't going to be nothing but a hoe like your momma."

I'd expect those words from an enemy, and probably

Damaged *Goods*

could've tolerated them a lot better from a complete stranger, but not my grandmother. Not my family. Imagine how hearing those poisonous words repeatedly throughout your life.

Now imagine the wounds coming from the hands of your own blood.

I tried convincing myself my grandmother's nasty words meant nothing to me. That she was a bitter, unhappy woman whose misery wouldn't drag me down. At least that's what I told myself.

"I'll show her," I said. "I'll prove I'm not who she says I am, I'm special and valuable and all things good."

I tried so hard to make myself believe my words over my grandmother's, but it didn't work. She got to me and over time, I began acting out at home, starting with disrespecting my grandparents. I started disrespecting my grandparents. Mom may not have been the best role model, but she never tolerated disrespecting our elders. I knew I wasn't raised the way I was behaving.

My disrespect wasn't only geared towards my grandparents. I disrespected any family member who tried to tell me what to do; no one could tell me anything. They didn't know how I felt or what happened to me, and weren't in any position to discipline me.

There were many times I thought of telling someone what I was going through, but I knew somehow it would backfire on me. If I told my family about the sexual abuse, their response would've been that I asked for it. After all, grandmother made it clear how she felt about me, and the family followed suit. I'd been hurt enough; the thought of sharing something so painful, only to get kicked down, was too much for me to bear. So, I kept my mouth closed and secrets tucked safely within.

You know life's bad when death feels like the best alternative. However, suicide is where I eventually found myself searching for a way out. I hated life; hurt like hell and

I no longer liked living. Yes, death was a permanent decision and if I was successful, it couldn't be undone.

Even knowing this, I made the choice to try.

It was a typical day for me. Nothing out of the ordinary had taken place, but I was tired and drained. I knew no one would miss me, because they were consumed with their own lives. After school, sitting in the living room with my sister and her boyfriend, I impulsively mentioned that I was planning to overdose on pills. Thinking I was joking, they brushed off my cry for help. I was furious. Tired of being taken for granted and as a joke. I'd show them. I'd show everyone.

I stormed away and grabbed the aspirin from the china closet in the living room. The directions on the back of the bottle stated not to take more than 12 aspirin within 24 hours, which meant I had to take down 12 or more aspirin to end the pain. Too bad for me, there were only six pills in the bottle. Undeterred, I swallowed everything in the bottle and reported what I'd done to my sister and her boyfriend. They examined the empty bottle to see if I was telling the truth, then said, "Girl you're crazy." I suppose at that moment, I was. I didn't second guess my decision or have doubts about it.

All I had to do was wait to die.

I lay on my bed, fantasizing about someone discovering my lifeless body, and how awful everyone would feel when I didn't wake up, finally forced to pay attention to me. I longed for the exact moment when I'd no longer suffer in silence and be ignored out loud.

Finally, my eyes grew heavy and I drifted off, slowly slipping into that peaceful place I longed for. To my dismay, after hours of deep sleeping, I woke up. Right back in the place I tried to escape. I didn't try to figure out why my attempt to die failed or question myself. I chalked it up to not taking enough pills. It was my first and only suicide attempt; death never crossed my mind again. No one really knew what

Damaged *Goods*

I'd done other than my sister and her boyfriend.
Family was still family.
My life was still hell.

Suicide is a serious thing. When I tried it, suicide wasn't taken as seriously as it is now. Sometimes it still isn't. BUT it is serious. Suicide attempts aren't always a play for attention. Often, it's because a depressed person just doesn't feel like living anymore, especially when life feels like it's all crashing down on you.

I'm glad I failed to die, so that I can live. I didn't have any regrets back then, and I don't have any now. I had to learn that everything happens for a reason. Had I succeeded, I wouldn't have my son and I wouldn't have met some amazing people, but most importantly, I would've aborted my purpose.

Masked

Seconds, minutes, days, and years went by…school still wasn't for me. I was an average student, doing enough to pass each grade and to get by.

I've heard to fake it 'til you make it. Well, I did that and more. I "faked" so well, I transformed into a completely different version of who I really was. There were two versions of me: the person I presented to the world, and who I really was. See, external faking is easy, because people only know what you allow them to know about you. Who they see is what they believe. Faking it for the world was the easy part.

Convincing myself was a different story.

There's no safe way to suppress the real you and put on a show for the world. Doing that very thing eventually tore me apart. Imagine if an actor is, "From now on, you're no longer yourself. From this day forward, you are to play the role you've been playing on set and off set." How difficult that would be? How much work it would take to stay in character, knowing it's not who you really are?

Damaged *Goods*

That was me.

There were times when everything felt right, but suddenly, out of nowhere, I'd burst into tears while performing the most mundane tasks. For instance, I' be driving, thinking about nothing in particular and when tears would start streaming down my face. Caught off guard, I would quickly swipe them away, especially when riding with someone.

I dreaded being asked if I was okay. Because it out trigger the floodgates, and I didn't want to keep crying. Not to mention, attempting to explain my feelings unleashed the, ugly cry. You know the cry people try to avoid displaying in front of others. It's so bad, it can't be seen outside of home.

I had an image to protect, at home and at school, so I didn't have time to cry. There was no time to feel pampered; I had to be strong. The one thing I wanted to avoid was people viewing me as weak, and by my estimation, tears were a clear sign of weakness.

I refused to cry.

My strength poured through my words and my attitude. I wasn't a quiet girl and didn't care what came out of my big mouth. I was just being me. Well... the pretend version of me. The one who didn't care how my words affected others, and stayed in defense mode. I was the girl who hurt people before they have a chance to hurt me. And if they couldn't handle me the way I was, then it was best for them to stay away. I had to look out for me, which no one else bothered to do.

When you're hurting, you don't care who you hurt. I became the hurt person willing to hurt anyone who crossed my path. Why care about other people's feelings when no one cared about mine? After all, no one cared about my innocence being snatched, or that I nearly died alone. Twice. No one was there for me. So, I treated others in the way that was familiar to me, from a place of hurt and anger.

I morphed into a walking billboard that read, HURT LIVES HERE. However, even though I was so mean and hurtful to others, I still managed to cultivate a number of friendships. A few friends did take the time to talk to me about my poor attitude, but none of them eve thought to ask me why I acted the way I did? Don't get me wrong, I don't blame my friends for not digging deeper to get to the root of the problem, since they weren't licensed therapists. Shoot, they were young and naïve just like me, and oblivious to my need for someone to pick up that something wrong.

My behavior wasn't normal, and I needed someone… anyone… to recognize my cry for help. I know it sounds confusing; believe me, I get it. On one hand I hid my pain so no one would ask about it; on the other hand, I was desperate for someone to ask what was wrong. I wanted someone to strike up the conversation, but I didn't want my tears to be what started it.

It wasn't fair for me to expect my friends to do what my own family couldn't. They complained about my behavior too, yet no one attempted to see what was really bothering me.

"You need to work on your attitude," my sister preached time and time again. "No one wants to be around you with that attitude".

My response was nonchalant. "So what? I don't need them."

I really believed it, too.

The people I needed were the same ones who hurt me. Why let my guard down and leave myself vulnerable to pain? I didn't mind being by myself. Being along meant being safe. I craved safety. Since I already felt alone, I was used to it, anyway. If people didn't want to deal with me, it was their loss, not mine. I figured I was weaning

Damaged *Goods*

out the wrong people, and making room for the right ones. My true friends.

Losing people meant nothing to me. After all, I'd already lost the most important person of all…myself. I was so consumed with pain that it was hard for me to see any good in my life. I was existing but not living. It's important to be able to distinguish the two.

Existing is simply getting by in life, surviving through mediocrity. On the other hand, living is making each day count, doing what you like or love, and fulfilling your purpose one step at a time. My past refused to let me see beyond the hurt I endured. The pain is so heavy, it was hard to focus on my purpose. If anyone told me that everything I endured would be used for a greater purpose, I wouldn't have believed them or even cared. I was consumed with what I'd gone through and the people who had failed to protect me.

I was o hurt, I remained stagnant far too many years. Moving forward is stressful when you're stuck playing a role. Stuck being someone you're not. I stayed angry with my guard up, wielding my attitude as a weapon to push people away. In the midst of it all, my life detoured again, and as usual- I wasn't ready for the upheaval. All the things I buried deep inside were about to explode.

How to Love

"You had a lot of crooks try to steal your heart, never really had luck, couldn't never figure out how to love." (*Lil' Wayne-How to Love*).

These lyrics speak to me on a level I can't even describe. I didn't know how to love. Truth be told, I didn't even know what love was. My vision of love was never demonstrated nor reciprocated, so how was I supposed to love anyone else. In spite of my lack of knowledge, I tried to love, anyway. At least, I used the term loosely.

After realizing what I thought was love wasn't authentic, I redefined the word to work for me. For me, love was less about how someone made me feel, and more about what they did for me. If things didn't go my way and I didn't get what I wanted, then I decided that person didn't love me. I measured love by material things and timing. If it was really love, then I'd get what I wanted sooner rather than later. Patience wasn't my strongest quality.

Damaged *Goods*

    My naivety when it came to love heaped more burdens on me, and I was already crumbling beneath a mountain of them. Since I hadn't dealt with my childhood issues new hurt exacerbated past pain. I carried more dead weight than I could stand, but somehow, I kept moving.

    In 2003, my junior year of high school, I met whom I believed was the love of my life. It felt like magic, unlike anything I'd ever felt before. We spoke on the phone for hours about any and everything. Being around him gave me butterflies; he spoiled me with everything I asked for. He was the first person to buy me flowers. I didn't have transportation to get to work; even though some nights it was late and he had to be up early the next morning for school, my boyfriend would still pick me from work and take me home. I just knew it was because he loved me so much.

    This guy was kind and sweet, but I had a hard time showing my appreciation. Sometimes I would complain about the smallest things, but that didn't deter him from being with me. We spent a lot of time together and surprisingly, my grandfather allowed me to attend church with him and his family. I loved his family. They were what I felt a normal family should look like: loving and caring, and they treated me nicely. After a while, we discussed marriage, and I couldn't see my life with anyone but him. Our future was all planned out. Things were going to be perfect.

    After graduating from high school, I wanted to attend Northwestern University. Me and my best friend made plans to leave and start the next phase of our lives together. The thought of moving away was exciting, but I had to be realistic. I didn't have transportation and couldn't stand the thought of being stranded so far away from home. So instead of following my heart to Northwestern, I stayed home and attended Remington College. I often wonder how different my life would be had I gone to Northwestern. Of course, not leaving for school also meant not leaving my grandparent's house, which stung more than anything else.

Not only did I change my mind about schools, my major changed as well. I wanted a degree in paralegal studies, but Remington didn't offer that major so I switched to criminal justice. Whichever path I took, had to lead to me becoming a lawyer and being a voice for victims like me. I was desperate to do my part to aid in getting criminals locked up and safely away from innocent people. I wanted to do for the victims what no one did for me.

I wanted to help.

The summer before freshman year, my sister announced she was pregnant. Seeing her so happy made me happy. She had a man that she loved, and they were expecting a baby. I wasn't jealous of my sister, but I did long for the joy she was experiencing. I had a measure of happiness that I clung to, but things are different when you're in college and your boyfriend's still in high school. I wanted my own baby to love, and who'd love me unconditionally. Someone who wouldn't hurt me. Yes, a baby was what my aching heart was missing!

A child would deliver me from myself.

By the time school started, my relationship with my boyfriend dwindled away along with the time we spent together. I was settling into my new role as a college student and he was focused on enjoying his senior year of high school, sports, and work. Sometimes he would still pick me up from work, but we couldn't go on our late-night dates because he had school the next day. The person who was once there for me was no longer there was suddenly too busy for me.

I resented his hectic schedule, and all I could to make him notice me. I craved his attention, and I just wasn't getting it. Besides, how was I going to get what I ultimately desired if my boyfriend wasn't there?

I had to act fast.

"Let's have a baby," I suggested one evening.

"I'm not ready for a baby," he firmly replied.

Damaged *Goods*

Why didn't he want a baby as badly as I did? Our love should have been enough, but it wasn't. I wanted – no, I needed this baby. A child would keep us together, and I could finally be happy. But I was damaged, and I wasn't enough for him.

He made it clear that timing was the issue when it came to us having a baby, but all I heard was rejection. If he didn't want me, I knew someone else would.

There was a guy on campus I couldn't believe was actually paying me some attention, entertained and it wasn't long before we exchanged numbers. Our conversations weren't interesting at all, but I entertained him because he had time for me. He made me feel important.

I became so involved with this new guy, I barely answered my boyfriend's calls. I conjured up all kinds of excuses whenever he tried to see me, with no regret. With my birthday coming up I decided to do something different. Different meant brushing my boyfriend off, once again, and spending time with the new guy. We'd already decided that my special day would double as the day when we'd hook up. There were signs all around me, warning me that it wasn't a good idea, but I ignored each and everyone.

The first sign came when my sister's boyfriend called to say he wasn't going to school and couldn't give me a ride like he normally did. Instead of accepting that it wasn't meant to be and moving on, I set out to find another ride. Determined, I texted a mutual friend of ours and asked for a ride instead.

I believe whenever you're setting out to do something wrong or something that will hurt others, God not only speaks to you through your thoughts, but He also send roadblocks to deter you. That day, I was determined to overcome every hurdle blocking my goal. I was going to cheat on my man, no matter what. Well, my mission was accomplished. That day, I hurt someone I loved. My damage, damaged someone else. At first, I didn't see anything wrong with what I did, but my sister's boyfriend saw a lot wrong with it and got on me.

"You would want him to tell you, so you should tell him," he fussed.

I instantly felt guilty. It was a Friday and my boyfriend had a game that night. My timing was lousy, but I needed to clear my conscience.

"If you would've made time for me or gotten me pregnant like I asked, then none of this would have happened."

That was the excuse I gave my soon-to-be-ex after the game, projecting my infidelity unto him. I refused to be held accountable; he was going to take this beating, even though he did nothing to deserve how I treated him.

After my confession, our relationship was officially over. To make matters worse, the new guy stopped talking to me. On top of that, I heard that he was going around telling his friends what happened between us, not that I cared enough to be embarrassed. I hated that I hurt someone I loved for no good reason, but there was nothing I could do to fix the damage I'd done.

After that encounter, I became extremely promiscuous, disregarding what people said about me. Caring was ripped from my heart years ago, so why start again now? There was nothing to care about. Wanting love so badly, I searched for my worth in all the wrong places. Guys I met along the way spoke the language I wanted to hear. They pretended to like me and gave me the attention I yearned. It was all lies, but I was too broken to recognize it.

These random men did exactly as my molester had done: take advantage of my vulnerable state, and I allowed it. I read a message somewhere that says you have to teach people how to treat you. I didn't respect myself or my body, so I ended up teaching those men it was okay for them not to respect me, either. In some cases, after they'd gotten what they wanted from me, I never heard from them again. I was

Damaged *Goods*

so used to people dropping in and out of my life, a few more didn't bother me.

Months passed and it was finally time for my sister to have her baby. I was surprised to bump into my high school sweetheart coming to visit her in the hospital. We made small talk which led to giving our relationship a second chance. I was elated to be forgiven for cheating, to work things out. I really missed him, so it didn't take much convincing for me to say yes.

Once we reunited, I expected to feel happy and joyful, but I didn't anticipate shame to dampen our reunion. His family made it so difficult to move on; they were well aware of my tumble from grace and how bad I had hurt him before. I was judged and talked about every time we were together; it was impossible to be around them. The pressure got to me and I had no choice but to end the relationship.

I hated the thought of hurting him again, but what choice did I have? The worst part was that I still wanted to have his baby, and like before, he was dead set against it. So, I did what I'd become an expert at doing: I moved on.

Once my sister was discharged from the hospital, she moved out of our grandparent's house to begin her new life, leaving me devastated. We'd never been separated before. She was the one constant in my life, and I wasn't certain I'd manage without her. I understood why she had to leave, but it still didn't stop me from begging her to stay.

Our living conditions weren't the best, but at least we had a roof over our heads. I wanted that to be enough for her, but now my sister was responsible for another life. She couldn't just think of herself anymore. Her child deserved more. The loneliness I felt when she left was indescribable, but it wasn't the worst part of her departure. The worst part was taking the brunt of my grandfather's choice words by myself. I took advantage of every opportunity I had to stay with my sister and her boyfriend. Most days, I was with them all day and didn't go back home until it was time for bed.

Avoiding home was my constant for coping.

The next time I tried love came as I interviewed for a job with a telemarketing company. As I sat in the waiting room, a gentleman struck up a conversation with me. He was great company, but I didn't think much of our small talk. When my name was called, he told me good luck and that was that.

For the time being…

After the interview, my brother (who had tagged along), handed me a piece of paper.

"What's this?" I asked, assessing the note.

"Open it," my brother urged.

I unfolded the paper to find a phone number scribbled on it.

"The guy in the waiting room asked me to give it to you."

Since I had nothing to lose, I called him. Before long, we spoke on the phone and texted daily. After dating for three months, I texted him an unusual request. The same one I'd already twice been denied – I wanted a baby. My dream of having a child was still very much alive and this man seemed like the best option. He was stable and treated me well.

What more could I ask for?

A few months after my request, I discovered I was pregnant. I knew my body well enough to know there was a life growing inside of me. It didn't matter that I still had a cycle, or that every pregnancy test I'd taken came back negative.

"I am pregnant," I casually announced to him.

"Well, it's not mine," he responded nonchalantly.

I was devastated. How could he deny something so precious? How could he not want this baby as much as I did?

We broke up.

Unlike all my breakups in the past, this one really hurt; another layer of pain added to all the others I endured.

Being apart didn't last long, though.

Damaged *Goods*

Throughout our time together, we were on and off like a light switch. I spent most of my pregnancy in tears. I finally got what I'd dreamt of having for so long, and I couldn't even enjoy the experience because my child's father in denial and questioned my baby's paternity. The nice and sweet man who romances me for months, disappeared. Issues we hadn't previously faced appeared from nowhere. Needless to say, I suffered through an incredibly stressful pregnancy.

One night, things got really heated between us. My sister, my boyfriend, and I had gone to grab a bite to eat. I can't remember all the details, but the date ended against the wall, his hand wrapped around my neck.

I looked to my sister to jump in and help, but she didn't. First, this mad denied our child, then he choked me. I still stayed with him though, refusing to follow in Mom's single mother footsteps. My child was going to grow up with both of his parents, no matter what I had to endure to make it happen. My stubbornness made sense at that time, but looking back, it wasn't worth it. The one less this toxic relationship taught me was staying together for the child, only hurts them.

We were in a horrible place. When things were good, he was the best boyfriend I could ever imagine. I still didn't have a car, and he bought me one. No one had ever done something like that for me; I equated it to love. Buying me that car showed that even though he could be mean and sometimes abusive, he obviously loved me. He wouldn't buy a car for someone he didn't love… right?

The day I was induced, I couldn't wait to meet my baby. The ride to the hospital was a mixture of joy and loneliness. I tried calling my baby's father, but he didn't answer the phone. He lived with his parents, so I called him there. His sister answered the phone, aggravation drenching her tone. Her groggy voice indicated she'd been asleep, but I told her what was happening, anyway and prayed she'd give him the message so he could get to the hospital before the baby came.

I was admitted and settled into a room where I waited with my sister and aunt. The doctors had given me medication to dull the extreme pain, and I was feeling good. Soon enough, I was knocked out.

I woke up to my baby crying and my boyfriend sleeping on the other side of the room. With staples in my belly, I struggled to raise up and get my son. The pain didn't matter. I just wanted to hold my baby. Giving birth to him was one of my proudest moments in my life.

That day meant more than birthing baby boy; I birthed a human who'd love me unconditionally. I birthed an innocent boy, who wasn't with me for ulterior motives or wanted to get what he could from me and leave. My child would change my life and teach me how to love. I vowed that day I would give my son the world. He'd have the best version of me.

The mother he needed and deserved.

Damaged *Goods*

Damaged Beyond Repair

Once a cheater always a cheater.
In my case, one damaged, always damaged.
Repairing my broken pieces seemed impossible. The lasting effects of the trouble I endured hovered over me like a dark cloud. I didn't know how to fix myself, and in all honesty, wasn't in a place where I wanted to be healed. It's one thing to want to be delivered, but another when you don't want to be. How can you expect others to help you when you don't want to help yourself? It doesn't make sense, but at the time I didn't want it to make sense. After all, everything that happened to me was my fault. I blamed myself for years.

If I would've said no all those years ago, maybe my molester would have stopped. Or if I told Mom, she could have stepped in and made him. I wish I'd told her, but was relieved that I ultimately decided not to confess. Because she'd believe me, which was actually the problem. If she had known that man was touching me, I would have been without both parents – because she would have killed him and gone to jail. Losing my mom to prison was more frightening than anything that man did to me.

There were many times when I thought of telling my sister what was happening, but I pushed aside the urge. I wasn't sure how she could help, and I didn't want her in the middle of my problems. I wished I had the courage to fight back.

People often wonder why victims don't come forth about the abuse or why it takes so long for them to speak out. Listen, rape and molestation aren't easy to admit. Sometimes, victims aren't ready to accept the truth themselves. It's almost as if saying it out loud or to anyone else, makes it real. The longer it stays inside, the longer the victim can continue pretending it didn't happen. No one will look at them funny or judge them like the damaged goods they are.

Who would willingly put themselves through that?

Truthfully, I couldn't say anything because I didn't want to accept my reality. My guardian molested me. The person my mother and I trusted did this to me. I also didn't want to accept it, and blamed myself. I never said no, and my silence gave him permission to do whatever he wanted to do with me. Yes, I was a child. Yes, he was grown and knew better, but, I still placed the blame at my own feet.

For years, no one knew. Not a single soul. I chose to deal with the battle on my own. And by dealing with it, I mean not dealing with it at all. I floated through life as if nothing happened, smiling on the outside, weeping inside. The funny thing about pain is that it never really goes away. You can dress it up and disguise, but it still doesn't leave. Not even if you ignore it and pretend it doesn't exist. Sooner or later, it shows back up. You can be living a great life, and then the pain silently creeps back in.

Before you know it, anxiety takes over your entire world.

Change isn't something that happens by a wish and a prayer; it requires action. It requires work…. hard work.

Damaged *Goods*

After birthing my son, I hoped things would get better between his father and me. My hope faded when I realized he was no longer the man I placed on a pedestal. My intuition worked well, leading me to suspect he was cheating. The gut feeling wasn't enough for me, though. I needed proof. And before long, I found exactly what I needed.

Seek and ye shall find.

That's what the Bible tells us to do, and that's exactly what I did.

One day, I searched his phone, and just as I suspected, the evidence I'd been looking for was right there. The time came for me to pack my things and put an end to our relationship once and for all, which would've been the logical thing to do, but on the contrary – that's not what I did.

I confronted him and cried; he apologized, and I accepted. I forgave him for his infidelities more that I care to remember, and forgave him for much more. Like the time I planned an outing with some friends from work. Of course, I couldn't confirm my plans until I discussed them with my son's father. After work, he waited in the parking lot for me, as he always did when he used my car. On the way to his mother's house, I told him my plans to hang out with friends, and I needed him to watch our son, which didn't sit well with him at all.

We argued furiously. In the midst of the fight, something inside of me snapped and I couldn't take it anymore. When we reached a red light and stopped, I jumped out the car and ran. He caught up with me at a gas station and hopped out the car, evil in his eyes. He grabbed my hair, and dragged me back to the car. People stood by watching, but no one stepped in to help me. Maybe they feared interfering like my sister did.

I didn't have the energy to keep fighting back, so I stopped. He shoved me in the car, and we drove off. Once we made it to his mother's house, I was emotionally and physically drained. I sat in the car, unable to move. I just needed to be still for a minute. I never did make it out with my friends that night, but he did. He went out and enjoyed himself while I stayed behind and dealt with the aftermath of his abuse. That was one of many physical battles we had. It was also one of many times I chose to stay when I shouldn't have.

I wanted to make us work for my son.

Eventually, things got so bad between us, I had no choice but to leave. I fled Baton Rouge and moved back to Lottie, Louisiana - a small town in Pointe Coupee Parish, the last place I wanted to live. I was angry, hurt, and spent nights praying for my son's father. I knew how to pray, and understood the power of prayer, but on those nights, I used prayer the wrong way. I wasn't praying for his good; I prayed he'd feel all the pain he inflicted on me and more. One night, I thought my prayer had been answered, but I now know that's not how God operates.

That particular night, my son ran a high fever. I was once again without a car and had no choice but to call my ex for help. Had I known he'd been out drinking with his friends all night and would bring a friend, one I didn't like, along with him, I would've found another ride. But, he was there, and my son needed to get to the hospital, so I didn't have time to be picky.

Just as we made it into Baton Rouge, my ex's car caught on fire. We made it safely out, and stood watching in shock as the car engulfed in flames.

Yes, God – You got him back for me, I thought.

I know it wasn't right, but neither was I and neither were the things he'd put me through. We called his to come get us to the hospital, and made it in time to get our son help.

Time passed, and like always we found our way back to each other. This go around, we decided we'd really try to make our family work. We moved back in together and for a while, life was good. We even had regular family night. For the first time I felt like things were going to work out for us,

Damaged *Goods*

and my son would have the life I never had. I was happier than I'd been in a very long time; so, I was devastated when things soured at lightning speed.

It started the night he climbed on top of me, accusing me of messing with someone else, which of course provoked another argument. He wasted my time, interrupted my rest, and disturbed my peace for nothing. When the dust settled, I mentioned my plans to return to school and finish my studies. He shot me down because I didn't have anyone to watch our son, and he wasn't going to do it. He didn't support my desire to make a better life for us. And as if things couldn't get any worse, they did.

Family night was about to begin. We were drinking-Hypnotic, and didn't even get to the fun part of the evening before arguing started and things quickly escalated. I can't recall what triggered the argument, but it shouldn't have happened. Instead of laughing and playing, we were physically fighting. He jumped on top of me, slapping me over and over in the face. In retaliation, I talked to him like trash. The more I talked, the harder he slapped.

I thought about running to the kitchen and grabbing a knife to let the night end one of two ways; one of us was going to kill the other while the murder went to jail. Either way, my son would be left without me.

It was time for me to go.

I finally reached a level of exhaustion that changed my life. I was tired of the fighting. Tired of the lack of support. Tired of broken promises. Tired of it all. Our situation was toxic; my mind was made up. I broke our lease and escaped. This time, moving back to Lottie didn't feel like a punishment. It felt like freedom.

I was losing myself in order to keep him, willing to sacrifice it all so we could be together. I'm thankful that I woke up and for the first time in my life, and chose me. I was damaged, but not beyond repair. I just had to do the work.

Total Knock Out (TKO)

Just when you think you're winning and on the right track, the devil steps in to tempt you. After my breakup from my child's father, I believed I was in a better place, thinking I was healed. Little did I know taking two steps forward eventually led to too many steps back when it came to me and relationships.

I was never shy when it came to approaching men. I know many ladies feel it's the man's job to make the first move, but I've never been one to sit back and wait on what I want, including men. I figured all we could do was get to know each other and if they didn't want to, I'd be okay either way.

One particular day, I took my son to football practice. On the way, I stopped at a store and ran inside for drinks. Standing in line to check out, I was instantly drawn to the cashier. He was a handsome, fair skinned man, who was so busy ringing up my items, he didn't pay much attention to me.

"Anything else?" he asked, glancing at me for the first time.

Damaged *Goods*

Everything in me screamed, *Yes! You can give me your number,* but I simply answered, "No, that will be all."

No matter how hard I tried, I couldn't stop thinking about that man. I dropped my son off at practice and headed back to the store. I wouldn't be satisfied until I at least tried to make a connection with him.

When I got back to the store, he was nowhere to be found. Discouraged, I left thinking I missed my opportunity, but it turned out I hadn't. Walking back to my car, I saw him exiting from the side of the building. Obviously, we were meant to be! I quickly raced over to him.

"Excuse me," I said as I approached him. "Can I talk to you for a second?"

"Sure," he said with a smile.

I wasted no time getting straight to business. "Do you have a girlfriend?"

"No."

"Good, then can I have your phone number?"

He grinned and answered, "Yeah"

We exchanged numbers and it started from there, and ended in yet – another emotional roller coaster.

No matter how bad things got, I wanted for us to work so badly, I was willing to do whatever it took to make it happen. In previous relationships, I ignored the red flags screaming at me to get out, this time, there were no red flags.

We texted periodically, which became all the time. When we weren't texting, we'd meet at our special spot. Our first date was simple, yet romantic. We traveled downtown to the levee, and spent time talking and getting to know each other better. As we talked, he mentioned a text message I sent him about the two of us kissing. I'm sure he expected me to shy away, but that wasn't me. I believed in backing up anything I said, and that's what I did.

I leaned close and kissed him. Feeling his lips against mine felt magical. We talked a while longer until we decided it was time to leave. The passion between us was electrifying; we couldn't keep our hands off each other. Standing next to my car, I jumped in his arms and wrapped my legs around his waist. He held me as we kissed, and it felt like a movie with him as my leading man. This was like nothing I'd ever felt before.

This relationship was going to be different.

I fell fast.

Six months passed and I was in love. But when I confessed my feelings, he couldn't reciprocate. Amazingly, I was fine with that. I didn't want him to express his love for me until he knew without a doubt he loved me the way I loved him.

I respected him for not throwing around the "L" word freely like so many others do and I appreciated honesty. He didn't lead me on. After all, he could've just lied to get what he wanted form me. He was completely different from other men I'd dated, and I welcomed that change. The day he finally uttered the words, "I love you," was so special. He expressed his love often. Our relationship was just as I had hoped it would be, until it wasn't anymore.

Things eventually got rocky; we both played a role in the demise of our relationship. For my part, I was extremely clingy. I craved all of his time, and didn't want him to be anywhere beside with me. This included infringing on his family time. Even though family was important to him, I was too selfish to care. He needed to be with me and my son. My son really liked him, and his approval made me feel we were becoming family.

Not only was I clingy, I was also quick to end our relationship if he didn't respond the way I wanted, which was often. He didn't give in easily and let me have my way, which ironically, was one of the things I loved and admired about him. He stood his ground and continued doing what he believed was right, like spending time with his family and friends. For me, this was a problem.

Damaged *Goods*

I failed to see that spending time away from me or not giving me what I wanted didn't cancel his love, but to me, every denial meant he didn't love me. By my standards, love was what he did for me. God says in His word, "Love is patient, love is kind. It does not envy, it does not boast, it is not proud. It is not rude, it is not self-seeking, it is not easily angered, it keeps no record of wrongs. Love does not delight in evil but rejoices with the truth. It always protects, always trusts, always hopes, always perseveres. Love never fails." (***1 Corinthians 13:4-8***)."

I was operating in a spirit of selfishness.

My shenanigans finally backfired on me in 2014.

It was Easter Sunday and I planned for us to spend the day together, yet – he wanted to spend the day with his family. Since his stepmother made it clear she didn't like us together and felt he'd be better off with a woman without a child and fewer responsibilities than I had, that meant I wasn't welcome at her house. Knowing she felt that way, I avoided being around her whenever possible. Easter together wasn't an option for me.

He chose to spend the holiday with his family, excluding me from his plans, so I did what I did best – broke up with him.

Again.

I thought this time would turn out the way all of our breakups did. We'd stop talking, then reconcile. That was our pattern; this time he broke the routine. I called him all that day and he ignored every call. Later that night, I called again from work. He answered this time, but as soon as he heard my voice, he hung up. I was crushed. This wasn't how the situation was supposed to play out. It felt like the end for us, but it wasn't.

Not yet.

I was clueless how stressed he was and how much he dealt with; my pressuring him didn't relieve his stress any. Sometimes, we have to focus on our significant others as well as ourselves. It isn't always about us and what we want. Our significant others have as much stress as we do – we have to recognize that. There may be times when they don't communicate what they're going through, but silence doesn't mean burdens don't exist. We have to pay attention to both what's being said and what's not being said. Pay attention to the clues.

We started dating again, but not before he made it clear that we weren't going to keep going back and forth. I knew he meant it, so I stopped breaking up with him every time I didn't get my way. That didn't mean I liked it, but I did what I needed to do to stay together.

Life was again going well and back on track. I learned how to bite my tongue most of the time and tried to accept that I wasn't the only one who loved and wanted to be around him. As his graduation approached, there was no way he wouldn't share his special day with his family. I was there every step of the way and was too proud of him to even consider not being there. Even having to deal with his stepmother. The good news was, I would finally get to meet his mother.

Graduation day finally arrived and I had the perfect dress, the perfect shoes, and of course my hair was slayed. My first assignment that day was to pick his mother up from the airport. Unlike his stepmother, his biological mother was sweet. At first, it was awkward being around his family because I didn't know if they shared the same feelings as his stepmother. Thankfully, they didn't. They eased my anxiety and made my son and I feel welcomed. They treated us like family and I wanted the feeling to last forever. I wanted my relationship to last forever.

I heard wedding bells…but they didn't ring long.

One night, his apartment complex caught fire. He had two choices; move back to his stepmother and father's house or move in with my son and me. He chose us and I could not

Damaged *Goods*

have been happier. Except… I forgot that living with someone, other than my son, wasn't easy.

Moving in together was different experience for us, but I was grateful he was with me, even if it was temporary. The more time we spent together, the more I wanted our temporary situation to become permanent. I didn't see the purpose of him looking for another apartment, since we were together. I loved the living arrangements, but he was determined to get his own place.

The time was approaching for him to move out and I noticed his demeanor changed. He was distant, and hanging with his friends more than usual. I worked long hours, so when I was off I wanted to spend my downtime with him. Unlike him, I didn't hang with my friends that often. I lost my identity outside of our relationship; I was his girlfriend and a working mother. Those were my roles, and I didn't deviate from them.

As much as I pretended it wasn't true, our relationship was on a downward spiral. The flame we once had was slowly extinguished. How we ended up in such a terrible place, I wasn't sure. I mean, we celebrated birthdays, were looking forward to the holidays together, and preparing to celebrate our 2-year anniversary. I thought we were in a good place.

I couldn't have been more wrong.

Despite everything, I still fought for us. He moved anyway. The fact that his stepmother helped him find another apartment crushed me; I could only imaging how elated she was to help him move away from me. What hurt most was the fact that he kept turning to the one person who he knew couldn't stand me for help.

Counting down the days to his move, I was depressed. I tried suppressing my disappointment and be as supportive as I could, but it was only so long before my frustrations exploded.

One Sunday while we were eating brunch after church, we argued. I cried nonstop, and kept excusing myself from the table so my son wouldn't see me so upset. I kept excusing myself from the table and going to the bathroom so my son would not see me so upset. I made frequent trips to the bathroom to compose myself as best as I could before returning to the table. The rest of the brunch and the ride home were uncomfortably silent.

When we pulled into the parking lot of the apartments, I couldn't get out the car without asking one last question.

"Do you really believe that I'm the one for you?"

He reassured me that I was, but something in his tone left me feeling unconvinced.

After seeing us safely inside, he returned to his father's house. The next time I saw him, we went into my room and prayed. Prayer works, but it only works within the will of God. Our relationship was over. The hardest part about the break-up was telling my son, who adored my boyfriend. Over two year, the two men in my life formed an amazing bond; my son was going to be devastated.

We played a game of UNO to ease the tension before dropping the bomb on my son. I barely got through that game; just like at the restaurant, I excused myself and went to the bathroom several times, sobbing. My world shattered once again. What was I going to do without him? He and my son were my entire world for so long, it made me sick that it was ending.

We were no longer together, but didn't move out immediately and spent most of his time hanging with friends and family until his apartment was ready. We went from being two people in love, to roommates who barely spoke. Our breakup was the worst heartbreak I'd ever experienced. Though my heart ached as if it was being ripped out, I continued going to work with my brave face, counseling others when I didn't even know how I'd carry on.

"What's wrong?" My clients would ask.

Damaged *Goods*

"Nothing. I'm just tired," I lied.

While struggling to keep going, it seemed like he was doing fine. His apartment was finished, and he moved out. After he was gone, we'd still text from time to time, but eventually he stopped responding. It hurt more to see him not sharing my misery. Didn't miss me. Wasn't suffering. Wasn't in pain. His happiness made me so angry. Angry with him for suggesting that we break up. Angry with his stepmother for filling his head with doubt about our relationship. Angry she convinced him he couldn't handle me and my child.

I hoped we'd get back together, but that fizzled by Christmas. It was the first Christmas since we met we hadn't spent together. I texted him, but his response wasn't what I wanted. It was evident that he didn't want to be bothered, so there I was again, a total wreck. I maneuvered through the holiday in pain. My son was at my sister's house and I was alone. I cooked gumbo and drank enough to numb my pain, but unfortunately, I did it on an empty stomach. Naturally, I made myself sick.

Sick and tired.

Once I felt better, I browsed some family pictures we'd taken and became furious. The more I traveled down memory lane, the angrier I became. I ripped up the photos, but it wasn't nearly enough damage, so I hauled the shredded pieces to the bathroom, tossed them in the sink and struck a match. I watched our memories burn to ashes. I wanted to see him burn. I wanted to see him hurt like I was hurting. Since burning him was out of the question, I did the next best thing.

Now, I didn't completely think my plan through before I jumped into executing it. My apartment was filled with smoke, and I was left empty. I took pictures of what I'd done and sent them to two of my friends, who raced to my apartment took me for a ride to get me out of the house. I was thankful for them, but not so thankful to return to a smoky apartment. I gathered some clothes for my son and me and stayed with my sister until the smell was gone.

I tried to convince myself I was done and had gotten him out of my system, but I was lying to myself. I didn't stop trying to find ways to be together. I didn't like being alone, and didn't want to be with anyone else, just him. Couldn't envision life without him. Besides my son, he was the best thing that ever happened to me.

Early into the New Year, we weren't back together, but I assumed he'd still be there for me if I needed him.

He proved me wrong.

One night, I received a text that my best friend was in the hospital and I rushed to be by her side. On my way there, I ran out of gas. He was the first person I called.

"Hello," he answered, with loud music blasting in the background.

"Are you busy?" I asked.

"Yes," he responded.

"I ran out of gas and I'm stuck on the side of the road."

I waited for him to say he'd come rescue me, but he didn't.

"I'm busy," he repeated. "And I don't have any gas money."

"I have money," I argued. "I just need you to come and get it then get me some gas."

He never showed up to help me.

My friend's boyfriend came and made sure I got to the hospital, where I stayed with her for a while. On the ride home, something hit my spirit and I ended up texting him again.

"I love you, but I love me more."

I was tired of trying to make it work when it was clear that he wasn't interested. He was living his best life, which didn't include me. I deserved better than crying while he lived. I was tired of hurting while he moved on so easily. The last time he abandoned me was the moment the version of me

Damaged *Goods*

that catered to the fantasy of happily ever after with him died. It was time for the new me to be resurrected. No matter how long it took, I was determined to defeat the old me. It wasn't easy, and there were many rounds to fight, but in the end the new me won.

It was a total knockout.

Blessings in Disguise

That final blow to our relationship was all I needed to discover who I was destined to be. God is so strategic in what He does. It was difficult to see myself bouncing back from that break up; however, my life took a positive unexpected turn. I'm so glad God knew what He was doing with me, because I was clueless.

At the point where it seemed I was losing in every area of my life, God showed me my life was just beginning. Not the life I created for myself, but the life He created for me. My life shifted in an unexpected direction. For the first time since I entered my first real relationship, I was single. I thought I'd be married and have more kids, but that wasn't the plan God had for me.

All of the damage and all of the pain had a purpose. Looking back, all the trails I endured were worth it.

Following the last breakup, God reminded me I still had a son who needed me. Not only that, God who loved me. That's the charge I needed to keep going but what really allowed me to pick myself up was understanding that I still

Damaged *Goods*

had ME. Did I have all the answers? Absolutely not. I wasn't sure what direction to go in or which step to take next, but I knew I had to find myself. Once I committed to finding me, things started changing.

One day at McKinley Middle School, a woman approached me following a counseling session in the library.

"Are you a licensed therapist?" she asked.

"No ma'am, but I do have a Master's in psychology."

"You need to get licensed," she responded. "I teach classes at Southern University."

I knew there was a reason why she gave me the information that day; her advice wasn't in vain.

Researching the program and its requirements, I learned that Louisiana was a social worker state. This meant that licensed professional counselors are not as recognized as the social workers are in the state of Louisiana. Social workers receive higher wages and more recognition than LPC's (licensed professional counselors).

In addition to my research on becoming a licensed therapist, I also dug into becoming a social worker. After gathering tons of information and weighing my options, I decided to take the GRE with plans to apple to the LSU social work program once I passed. Why LSU? Because living in Louisiana would benefit me in obtaining the degree I needed. After taking the test and receiving my results, I called LSU to verify their requirements.

"Can you tell me the GRE scores needed to apply for LSU?" I excitedly asked the administrator who answered my call.

She verified the scores I needed to be considered for acceptance, and to my disappointment, mine were too low.

"Okay, I'll just take the test again," I said, trying to remain optimistic. Unfortunately, the woman didn't share the same optimism.

"Just because you take the test again doesn't mean that you get accepted into LSU."

I don't know if she intended to deter me from applying or if she was just stating the facts, but either way, I didn't allow her negativity to get me down.

"Okay, thank you," I responded politely.

Honestly, that wasn't the response I wanted to give; however, when God is working on you, He'll cause you to handle things differently. Even though I pretended she didn't get to me, I couldn't stop thinking about what she said, letting doubt creep in.

I reminded myself not getting into LSU meant that God had better plans for me. I'd proven to myself that I didn't know what was best for me, but God does. And I stuck by that. He can see the things I can't.

I realized I really didn't want to attend LSU. If the attitude of that woman reflected the staff and values of the school, it wasn't the place for me. I had a choice. And I'd enough of settling for things and people because they looked good. Nope not this time. I applied for Southern University instead and was immediately accepted.

But God!

In August 2015, I entered Southern's Masters program for Clinical Mental Health Counseling. This was just the start. I was already balancing working full time, two part time jobs, and motherhood… now I went and added being a student, too? I must have been crazy.

But sometimes, crazy births purpose.

For the first time, my life looked bright. I clearly saw what I could accomplish and hungered for more. My next goal was to purchase a house, so my son and I moved in with my sister. Living with her was a blessing because I was able to work all of my jobs, without worrying about finding someone to take care of my son and save money.

Now I can't pretend the struggle was over. It was a constant fight not to throw in the towel and walked away from it all. My schedule was jam-packed and I was completely overwhelmed, but giving up wasn't an option.

Damaged *Goods*

My son needed me. And he watched me closely. My moves from then on out had to be good ones.

Finding Me...

In June 2015, I attended our church's women's retreat. We were there a few days, with no television and poor phone reception but it was just what I needed. Once again, God knew what I needed, and He provided. I experienced a mighty move of God. Healing took place.

I opened up about feeling abandoned as a child, then there was an awesome exercise where everyone's name was printed on posters and hung on the walls. We went around the room, writing positive things about the other women on their poster, and it was incredibly powerful.

That day, I learned people saw something in me that I didn't see in myself. Who knew my smile meant something to someone else? I didn't think anyone paid attention to my smile. They saw me as a good mother, and called me strong.

If only they knew.

I didn't feel strong, but seeing such positive words strengthened me. The affirmations played a major part in my healing.

Damaged *Goods*

The retreat blessed me in so many ways. We were given positive affirmation cards to take home, a guest pastor preached mightily and prophesied over us, and my first lady prophesized over me and others.

Life would never be the same.

The good feeling I had after leaving the retreat was overshadowed by a new worry: how to come up with the closing costs for my new home. Even with three jobs, I didn't have the money and was scared I wouldn't get it. But I hadn't made it that far not to get the house that I dreamt of. But it was hard for me to ask anyone for anything. Not because I didn't want to, but because I didn't want to hear "no". I don't like hearing no, which is crazy, because I don't mind saying it.

No brings on disappointment. I heard it so many times through the years, it stripped my expectations off people. Expecting someone to do something for you because you'd do it for others, won't make them do it. I put my pride aside, I laid my expectations down, and asked for help.

I called my uncle for the money to cover my closing costs. He said he'd have to get back to me after he spoke to his accountant, better known as his wife. I thought for sure I was doomed; my uncle doesn't lend out that kind of money to our side of the family. But to my surprise, he said yes! I promised to pay him back once I received my taxes the following year.

I was excited. My son and I were about to have our own home, and were well on our way. I was active in church and became co-leader of the church's book club, which was huge for me. When I was first asked to think of books we could read, I thought of Zane (I wasn't thinking church books). But my partner really helped me, and played a vital part in my healing process.

She started by choosing some good books for us to read. These books taught me so much about myself, and I learned more about who God is. I was shown everything I went through had to happen. Where would I be without my damage? Where would I be without my pain? Would I still be the same person if I weren't molested? How would my life have turned out? All those questions swirled through my mind, and I don't have the answers for them. I can always wonder what if, but *what if* isn't my life. *What if* didn't get me where I am today.

God did.

Damage shaped me into who I am today. Genesis 50:20, mentions the devil's intentions are subject to God's will for my good. Every bit of my suffering was meant for good. I was bruised but for my good. Felt worthless, for my good. Questioning everything…but for my good.

It was all for my good.

I was scheduled to close August 17, 2015 and start school August 24. The week of closing, I mentioned another account that I had to the mortgage originator, which resulted in my closing date being pushed back a week to August 24, the same day school started. I couldn't enjoy closing day the way I wanted because I had to sign the papers and get to class. First day of school, and I was late. I can't stand being late.

I shook off first day frustrations, and tackled school head-on. I learned so much from all of my professors. First lesson – don't allow anyone say what you can't do. I didn't want to be in school forever, so I wanted to take 4- four classes my first semester. The program director said I couldn't though. After meeting with her, I convinced her to approve the class schedule, which I maintained for the duration of the program. I'm asked a lot how I did it. My answer? It was nobody but God. The motivation and determination He instilled in me. I was determined to finish what I started.

Second – Don't disqualify someone or a business based off of other's experience.

Damaged *Goods*

I'm well aware of complaints surrounding Southern University. How awful financial aid is, how rude some staff if, and how unorganized they are. While that could be true for some people, it wasn't the case for me. Sure, I encountered rude people, but it was up to me whether or not to let that hinder me or take it personal. I vented to my friends, but quickly brushed it off. My goals weren't worth sacrificing over petty things.

Thirdly – I learned although we experience issues, there's a blessing in the mess.

See, my professors didn't simply educate me... they schooled me about life. They made sure I knew no one owed me anything; life's what I make of it. Everyone endures pain, but not everyone heals from it. Healing is a choice: let the past define us or redefine us. I chose to reintroduce the better version of me.

I don't have to stay where I'm damaged. Southern taught me that things will not always go my way, however, I need patience, which Southern taught me – especially when the professor was tardy for class. Every day I gained more knowledge, growing stronger than I ever believed, finding my power in Christ. Even on my worst days when all I wanted to do was go home and jumped in bed after work, I pressed my way to class. It was all because of God.

Last, I met some amazing people I'm still connected to.

One of my colleagues turned into a bestie, which evolved into a sisterhood. She lifted me up, from assisting me with my pronunciation to providing scripture and motivation when I need it the most. She's held my hand through everything. I'm extremely thankful for all the Godly relationships I've gained over time. I'm also thankful for the struggle, because that's where I discovered my strength.

Everything meant to destroy me, God used to bless me. It's mind blowing, to think if we stop to process what's happening, we can recognize God's presence in the midst of it all. We're not alone, even when we believe we are. God is with us, carrying us through the storm. Often times, we want to be delivered from the storm, but God wants us to endure it, so we can GROW THROUGH it. We can't grow through anything if we haven't been through anything. Reflecting over my life, I'm grateful for all the trails that were blessings in disguise.

Damaged *Goods*

All of Me...

Have you ever questioned yourself? Of course, you have...we're not perfect. It's easy to question our mistakes; it's not so simple to forgive ourselves for them.

We often question ourselves and our actions, but how many of us can be honest enough to admit we've questioned God, too? During my valley experiences, I asked God "why" continuously, as I sank into a never-ending cycle of confusion.

It's one thing for you to be damaged, but it's an entirely different situation when people recognize you're damaged. It's easier for some to share their story than others, because we don't want to be labeled as broken. That was me. For the longest time, I didn't want anyone to know that I was damaged. Testifying about your truth makes it a reality, and you have to be ready to own it.

Aside from uncovering the reality they've desperately tried hiding, damage doesn't want to be judged. People don't easily allow someone else's torrid past to rest, constantly reminding them of the place they were delivered from. The person they've grown into gets confused with the person they were. And when someone finally gains the strength to walk away from their past, negative people claim they think they're "better" than them.

Growth turned toxic.

When we grow, the issue isn't putting ourselves on pedestals above everyone else; but we're above the issues that drug us down in the first place – and the ones who knew us "back then" are more comfortable keeping us in bondage. Everybody hasn't endured the same struggles. One person's struggle can be staying afloat in a single-parent household, while someone else's could be fighting to survive in a two-parent home. The circumstances are different for all us. Understanding this is the first step to stripping the labels off each other.

Judgmental labels create walls. And walls create a safe place for hurting people. Staying to themselves means being safe and protected from being hurt again. There's nothing wrong with that, but people like me shouldn't have to suffer in silence. Victims shouldn't be judged based on what's happened to them. The Bible even tells us judge not lest we be judged – which includes moving beyond the past where victims no longer live. And if by chance the victim has yet to move on, we can help them move forward, as they feel comfortable. God's the ultimate judge, not observers holding the mirror in our face.

We do better when we know to do better, but what happens if we don't know where to start? Everyone wasn't raised the same way. For instance – I never learned how to cook. I can either allow that to keep me from cooking or try to learn. Sometimes, we just need direction and guidance. We all need someone who believes in us. I needed someone to believe in me other than me, and for many years, I wasn't blessed with that someone. I knew I was capable, but without that voice of light, doubt creeped in more than faith. I was

Damaged *Goods*

scared to succeed because I didn't know what was next, and was always looking for the next best thing. I haven't embraced *right now* until now.

Purchasing my home in 2015 was so exciting! But instead of enjoying the blessing, I spent time pointing out the things in the house I wanted to fix. In my relationships, I was a fixer. In my friendships, I was a fixer. I tried my hardest to fix everything in my life, and that's where I went wrong. If I noticed a bit of damage or a little bruise, I wanted to fix it. The thing is, none of it was for me to fix. God didn't call me to fix anyone; He called me to do His will and serve His purpose. Serve His people by showing them the steps to healing. Starting with my own.

Embrace who YOU are.

Embrace the accomplishments you've made. Embrace the good, not the bad. Embrace the strongest parts of you, rather than the damage. See when you go to the ultimate healer, He will heal the damage and He makes you brand new. He'll heal you. He'll take your damage and make it your testimony.

I wouldn't wish what I've gone through on my worst enemy.

"Why me", I'd ask God.

I head the response clear as day: "Why not you? God went on to say, "My word says ALL things work together for those who love the Lord." "Donna do you love Me?"

"Of course," I replied. "Yes, God I do love you."

"Then trust Me. Know that I am working every trail and every tribulation out for your good. Yes, you have been damaged, but I am working it out for your good. I can still use you. Donna, I chose you."

Staying true to His promise, God worked everything out for my good. Every bad thing I believed was going to take me out, He BLOCKED. The molestation, the abuse, the hurt, the pain; all worked out for my good. God did it for me, I know He can do it for you, too. He'll turn your broken pieces into masterpieces. Your trials may have left you damaged, but God will carry you through the fire, and you'll be better than ever!

1 Peter 5:7, God say cast ALL your cares upon Him because He cares for you. His word doesn't say some cares, it says ALL of them. Transparency: I didn't follow God's word.

Listen, just because you experienced pain doesn't mean God wants you to carry it. He wants you to release it back to Him. He wants you to acknowledge it happened, accept that it did, and deal with it. The only way to deal with hurt is to give it back to God. Give to Him and forgive your offender.

Give the pain to God.

He said He would never put more on your than you can bear which means stop holding on to dead weight. Yes, it happened… but pain doesn't have to be permanent. God can turn our mess into a message and that test into a testimony. God can make all things new despite what we went through, but we must turn it over to Him. Choose to drop the dead weight. Choose to relinquish your rights to the pain. Give it back to God. He is the owner of it not you.

No matter how far along in life you get, sometimes doubt creeps back in. Have you ever downplayed yourself because you felt like you didn't deserve any good? I've been there. In times when I was filled with confidence, and others when I was unsure of myself. I used to stop myself from going after my dreams because I thought I didn't deserve anything because of my past. Sometimes people throw your past in your face; in my case I did it to myself. I was my own worst enemy, using my past as a weapon against my future. Although I was in a better place, I didn't allow myself to fully blossom in a better space.

Sometimes, we can hinder our own progression.

Some people wait a lifetime to be freed from themselves. I could've been one of those people and thrown in the towel. But I knew that wasn't what God wanted me to do. See, God

Damaged *Goods*

doesn't want us to give up when things get tough or when it seems like we have nowhere to turn or go. God wants us to trust Him. He wants us to call on Him so he can provide everything we need. God knows the end before the beginning. In spite of what we've gone through, God knew how it would all turn out. Just like He did for me.

God already knew I would win.

I've been knocked down time and time again. But just as many times as I have been knocked down, God helped me get right back up. The rough part of our journey isn't about getting knocked down, it's about getting back up and doing something about it. See, I chose to do something about my situation. We all have a choice. Choose to define your own happiness. Choose to dust yourself off again. Choose to pick yourself back up. Choose to live again. Choose to move in the best direction for you. It's complicated, but it's possible. All things are possible through Christ who strengthens me and you. All we have to do is take the first step toward change.

When we're knocked down, we have to position ourselves to stand again. God doesn't intend for us to be defeated. Jesus wasn't defeated – He was victorious. God wants us to be victorious, too. But in order to be victorious, we have to fight. We can't win if we don't swing. Faith without works is dead. Yes, God is on our side, but we have to put some work in too.

Getting up is for you. Healing is for you. Deliverance is for you. I'm here to testify that in spite of all the bad things that have happened to me, I am still victorious, and you can be too. What happened was not the end of you. The trial is just the beginning of who God was preparing you to be.

Who would've known I'd be where I am today? Sometimes, it amazes me. I truly believed I would've been taken out a long time ago, but I'm still standing. God's promises are Yes and Amen. He truly worked things out for my good.

Until Death Do Us Part

We have to love ourselves as God has loved us. Then others will be able to love us, too. Let me tell you, your value isn't diminished because your parents said you were a mistake. You're worthy, even when your father or mother walked away. You're not worthless because you're flawed. You're not downgraded because they walked out on you, you got fired from your job, contracted an STD or spent time in jail. You're priceless in spite of it all.

Sis, you're valuable. You're valuable to you. You're valuable to me. But most importantly, you are valuable to God. He is your creator. Remember God gave you value, and no one can take that away from you.

God gave us value when we were formed in our mother's womb. Do not allow society to define your value based off of how much money you make, the car you drive, your marital status, the degrees you have, etc. Stop giving "people" the satisfaction and start giving God the glory.

Damaged *Goods*

The Vows

Marriage is a big step in a relationship. People don't often see the pitfalls and triumphs couples experience before they're married, or during the marriage. Outsiders automatically assume the marriage is perfect – but that's based on what they see. All relationships encounter conflict. Especially when it comes to getting cold feet – having a doubt or strong urge not to go with something as planned. Some people experience cold feet as their wedding day approaches and they're unsure the person they're walking down the aisle is the person that they want to spend the rest of their life with. I've been that person. I've held myself back from being my authentic self – several times because I wanted to be accepted, not wanting others to dislike me.

When we get to the point of having cold feet, it's imperative to take a step back, and reassess some things and revisiting Gods word put things in perspective. Revisiting our roots (His word) helps us remember God promises. His word is protection, peace, love, and joy. It's present, everlasting, and true. We can take His word to the bank and cash it, for it won't return void. Once we dive in His word, we can nurture our seeds with positive thoughts.

Mental stability is key. If my mind isn't right how can anything else be right? Remain positive, even when it looks bad, and remain true.

The singer Lloyd was off the scene for a while, but he reassessed somethings, cut some people off, and released a song titled "Tru". My favorite part of the song says " This is me, so please accept me for who I am and please accept me for what I do. Lloyd goes on to say more about wanting to be TRUE.

This song resembles the place I'm at in my life. I no longer have cold feet. I no longer have the doubts like I used to. My doubts are passive, but can't stay. I'm sure that I want this to last forever. There is no me without God; I can't be true without Him. I'm nothing without Him. I must first acknowledge God in everything. He is first, because He loved me first. Our first vow ever should be to God. Our first *'till death do us part* shall be unto God.

As we have breath in our body, it's never too late. I have made a vow to God, now I must make one to myself. I'm not married or dating and that's okay. Marriage used to be my main focus. I planned and prepared; even went to the mall to pick out my won ring. It was all wrong timing. Through the course of my relationships, I've learned to wait on God. There's nothing like due season and the best part is, DUE SEASON HAS TO COME!!!

Damaged *Goods*

Vow to myself:

I Donna Barnes take you to be my partner for the rest of my life.
I take the good, the bad, the ugly
I take the past, the present, and the future.
I take the hurt and the joy.
I take the lonely nights and tears.
I vow to love you as God has loved you.
I vow to cherish you as God has instructed me to do so.
I vow to be the best mother I can be.
I vow to never let you go now that I have you
I vow to treat you with respect and love
I vow to meet you halfway.
I vow to honor you and engage in self-care practices.
I vow to never mistreat you
I vow to never cause any harm to you
I vow to love you when you are up and down
I vow to love you whether fat or skinny
I vow to love you with your morning breath
I vow to have compassion and empathy.
I vow to laugh at your jokes and make you smile.
I vow to see things in a positive light.
I vow to trust God that he will never start us in the wrong direction
I vow to help you whenever you need help
I view to put you first and be there when you need me.
I vow to be fully committed to you, learning with you, and growing with you.
I vow to lift you up when you have a bad day.
I vow to stand up for you but also let you know when you are wrong.
I vow to take you as you are, as the creator has made you.
I vow to accept you flaws and all.
I vow to be there every step of the way.

I vow to keep these vows on today
I vow to be me, accept me, whole heartedly
Lastly, I vow to not lose myself. I have found who I am, and I am embracing ALL OF ME.
I VOW TO WALK IN MY TRUTH, MY IDENTITY
I VOW TO BE ME…

Conclusion

This book isn't for self-pity, blame, or airing dirty laundry. These pages are filled with encouragement to show readers God's word is *Yes and Amen.* What He says shall come to pass.

You choose what you allow. I've been through hell and back, but I came out. I've been damaged, mentally and physically, even at my own hands. But there were also many good things that have transpired in my life. I just had to change my view.

Wearing dark glasses impedes perception. What can be seen in the dark? Darkness blurs our vision. Cleaning the lens to see the situation clearly keeps us from blindly believing obstacles won't happen. What we go through has to happen. Including the damage. Understand that you're no longer a victim… you're a VICTOR. You choose what you want to be called. I am a victor. I am a survivor. I am an overcomer.

Life happens.

We're not always dealt a fair hand, but we have to work with what we have. We can make the best out of the life we have been given. That's the part that counts. Make every day count; maximize the great moments, because you can't get time back. I could've easily held onto mistreatment and hurt, but it wouldn't have served any purpose or benefited me. I made up my mind to do something different. I chose to live and not exist. To be better, not bitter. But most importantly, I chose to acknowledge my worth. I'm still chosen, valued, and loved.

Damaged goods is defined as something that is broken, scratched, or a person who is no longer valuable or desirable. I can accept this definition, or I can rewrite it.

Guess what I choose to do?

I define "damaged goods" as someone who's been hurt, torn, and damaged, yet emerged as God's masterpieces. Damaged property, items, or people can still be used. God can still use us in spite of our chipped armor. The abuse, our track record, what others say about us, the suicide attempt, the abortion. No matter how awful we think our scars are, God still qualifies us – damaged and all. He still chooses us; qualifying the unqualified. Don't give up hope, and don't lose faith, because it can and will happen for you. Accept that you are still GOOD.

I was once broken, but I'm restored. I could've been taken out years ago, but God saw fit for me to remain. He still has a purpose for me. I was abused in every way possible but it could've been worse. I had to go through to birth this book for you. Without the storms and trails, I wouldn't be where I am today. The winds will blow; and the rain will fall but at the end of the day, I will stand tall.

Storms will rise again, but I will call on Jesus, my best friend. No matter how weary and tired I get, I'll catch my breath. My soul will be on fire for God. On fire to continue and not give up. I will conquer the storm and each one thereafter, because of my Father.

I may bend but I won't break.

Damaged *Goods*

I may have been damaged, but I'm good at the end of the day.

The damage didn't break me, it made me who I am today!!!

DAMAGED GOODS!!!

…for my good.

www.ingramcontent.com/pod-product-compliance
Lightning Source LLC
Chambersburg PA
CBHW071413290426
44108CB00014B/1807